[CODING YOUR PASSION™]

USING COMPUTER SCIENCE IN
DIGITAL GAMING
≫ CAREERS ≪

JENNIFER CULP

Rosen
YA™
New York

Published in 2018 by The Rosen Publishing Group, Inc.
29 East 21st Street, New York, NY 10010

Library of Congress Cataloging-in-Publication Data

Names: Culp, Jennifer, author.
Title: Using computer science in digital gaming careers /
Jennifer Culp.
Description: First edition. | New York : Rosen Publishing,
2018. | Series: Coding your passion | Includes bibliographical
references and index.
Identifiers: ISBN 9781508175223 (library bound)
Subjects: LCSH: Electronic games industry—Vocational guid-
ance. | Computer games—Vocational guidance.
Classification: LCC HD9993.E452 C85 2018 | DDC
794.8023—dc23

Manufactured in China

CONTENTS

INTRODUCTION

The term "digital games" encompasses a wide variety of programs that are playable on a diverse array of hardware. Digital games can be played on video game consoles, like those produced by Microsoft (Xbox) and Sony (PlayStation); user-customized desktop computers with advanced graphical capabilities; and even on cell phones! The games themselves vary enormously, too, ranging from very simple puzzle games and interactive choose-your-own-adventure visual novels to massive multiplayer online roleplaying epics. Babies and toddlers can enjoy playing simple games designed to challenge their developing motor skills, and older people can play games to stay connected with friends. Some people play digital games to take a vacation from the "real world" after getting home from work or to pass the time on the morning subway commute. Our world is saturated with digital games, and they serve a multitude of important purposes: distraction, education, imagination, and play. Whether frivolous or deeply emotionally affecting, digital games are an important part of modern life, and many people dedicate their careers to creating them.

"Code" is the series of instructions that tells a computer what to do. Code is made up of different programming languages that communicate with different machines. Just like your teachers give you instructions

Digital games also help people communicate with each other, offering a platform for competition, cooperation, and the thrill of exploring virtual spaces together.

in English, for example, programmers use languages with names like Python, JavaScript, C++, and UScript to talk to computers. Learning to code essentially means learning a new language—or languages—and how to use its syntax properly so that the computer can understand and carry out commands. Game engine programs like UnReal and Unity are software development tools used to simplify game building.

Game engines are equipped with complex prewritten code scripts to control the behavior of game environments and objects, allowing people who make digital games—game developers—to assemble complex games without having to write every single bit of the game's code from scratch.

Specialized skill sets allow for particular focus on the creation of different elements of digital games. The term "game developer" or "game dev" is used to refer to a whole host of different game creation jobs, but when it comes to large, complicated games, dev jobs can get very specific indeed.

Game designers dream up the gameplay mechanics, creating what's essentially the skeleton of a video game—its structure and mode of play. Narrative designers construct a game's story: plot, dialogue, characterization, and world-building information, directing the player's individual experience in an understandable and affecting fashion. Concept artists envision the look of a game's world, characters, environment, and objects, and technical artists manifest these visions in virtual spaces, aided by 3D modelers and texture artists. Level editors build and populate the environments players explore in a game, striking a precise balance of challenging and fun with clues, objects, obstacles, and enemy artificial intelligence. Audio engineers provide music and sound effects to affect the player's mood and experience of the game. DevOps engineers (people who create and maintain secure networks for online play) tackle the complicated, ever-evolving task of developing and maintaining secure networks for online gameplay, and programmers write the code that allows a game or even a game engine to function in the first place.

Small indie games might not require such a large team to assemble and are instead created by a small collaborative group of people who take on multiple development roles, or even by a single individual. Triple-A (AAA) game development studios may employ hundreds of people in order to complete expensive blockbuster console titles. Many people work to bring digital games to life, and with some education in pro-gramming and game design, you could become one of them.

CHAPTER ONE

GAMES AND PROGRAMMING

Computers are versatile tools capable of performing astounding feats of computation at high speed, but they don't "think" the same way human beings do. The computers used to build and run all digital games are, at their essence, machines that use patterns of fluctuating electrical voltage to perform arithmetic. The computer's "brainwaves," so to speak, are actually patterns of shifting voltage that the computer interprets as simple binary signals of "on" (0) or "off" (1). In order to communicate with a computer, humans combine these ons and offs—0s and 1s—into long and increasingly complex patterns that the computer can interpret as a vocabulary of commands. These commands may then be combined into processes that let the computer know how to perform even more intricate actions. As more and more processes are combined, the computer can do cooler and more complicated stuff.

```
32    if(item_Event == "RT_EVENT" and pivotCell==))
33    if(item_Event == "RT_EVENT" and pivotCell>=5):
34    else: if(str(cell.value) != "None"): value
35    if(item_Event == "RT_CHAIN_EVENT" and pivotCell==)
36    if(pivotCell%2 == 1 and str(cell.value) != "None")
37    pathOfTemplate = "templateFolder\\" + item_Template
38    if(item_Event == "RT_OUTPUT" and pivotCell>=4):
39
90    tempString = template_type_buffer tempString
91    dataCal = datetime.date.strftime(d, "%Y-%m-%d")
92  ⌐ tempString = tempString.replace("czDataType",
93  ⌐  elif(typeOfFID == "TIME"):  dataCal = str(value)
                Obj2 = re.search( r'(\d+)-(\d+)-(.*)
```

Machine code looks like a foreign language to the uninitiated...and that's because it is! Code is the native language of computers.

THE TOOLS

Machine code functions as the basic building blocks of computer language. However, creating an entire program—a set of instructions that tells the computer how to perform complicated tasks—would be very difficult for a human being to compose entirely in simple machine code. To accomplish the task more easily, people rely on a programming language to create sets of instructions for the computer. Then, another program translates the commands written in the programming language into source code the computer can more easily understand. To recap, a computer must be told exactly what to do in a language that it can understand: machine code. Increasingly complicated combinations of code are combined into different programming languages, which people use to write sets of complex instructions for the computer to follow. Then the computer uses a program to translate the instructions back into simple machine code it can easily understand and follow. This is, *very* basically, an explanation of how digital games are built: developers use a particular code-based programming language to write instructions that tell the computer how to represent game environments, perform actions, and how to react to the player's input. Another computer translates and executes the code, and voilà! It's a digital game.

There are two main types of programming when it comes to digital games: systems programming and web programming. Systems programming is used for what's called a "standalone application," like a video game you play on an Xbox console. Java and C++ are two programming languages commonly used for systems programming, and game building engines (which we'll discuss later) also often use these languages. Web programming is used to make games that run online over a web browser. Languages for web programming include HTML, CSS, JavaScript, and SQL.

There are thousands of programming languages, and a lot of them are used in programming games. Expensive, complicated AAA games you play on your PS4 might use many of them in different aspects of creation. So, which programming language is most commonly used in game development? Which language, or which set of languages, should an aspiring game developer set out to learn?

"To be honest I don't like this question, because it is a question I cannot answer," wrote *Super Meat Boy* developer Tommy Refenes in a blog post for the game development website Gamasutra in 2013. Refenes recommends doing some research to discover which language feels most comfortable to you to begin with, and start learning there. "Stick to what you know, or go the easiest, most comfortable route possible to acquiring skills to start work on your game. So if you know a little Flash, use Flash, if you use C++, use C++, if you only use Java, then use Java. There is no such thing as 'the official game development language.' ALWAYS remember that. *Minecraft* is written in Java, *Super Meat Boy* is written in C++, *Farmville* is written in Flash, some other game people play is written in HTML 5, some other game people play was made on index cards. The point is: It doesn't matter. Find a way you can make your game comfortably, and make it with that."

A good way to decide what programming language or development platforms you might start with is to take stock of games you particularly enjoy and look up the programming language or languages that were used in their creation. Alternatively, you could think about what type of game you'd most like to create and figure out which programming language is best for making it. The interactive Code Academy website is a free online service designed to teach programming languages including Java, HTML, CSS, SQL, PHP, Python, and Ruby (among others) to novices with absolutely no prior experience in coding. Companies such as Hackbright and Girls Make Games aim to redress the male-heavy gender imbalance in tech by offering coding education solely to women students. While Hackbright focuses on quickly furnishing adult women with professional entry-level programming skills for a significant tuition fee, LearnDistrict's Girls Make Games programs offer intro classes on game design, game art, and programming to young women at a much lower price point.

In 2010, President Obama announced the launch of the National STEM Video Game Challenge to motivate interest in science, technology, engineering, and math in young people of all genders. In 2016, the challenge

TYPES OF DIGITAL GAMES

There is an enormous variety of digital games!

- The apps on your phone, *KleptoCats*, *Blendoku*, and *Kim Kardashian: Hollywood*
- Desktop computer-based massively multi-player online roleplaying games like *World of Warcraft* and *Star Wars: The Old Republic*
- Free-to-play indie-created Flash games hosted online by services such as Kongregate
- Choose-your-own-adventure-style visual novels that allow a player to "romance" a fictional paramour like *otome* games

- Console platform games like those of the *Rayman, Mario, and Ratchet & Clank* franchises
- Button-combo mastery fighting games like *Street Fighter V*
- Kinect and PlayStation Move-enabled dance games like *Wii Yoga*
- First-person shooters like *Halo, Call of Duty, DOOM, Overwatch*
- Online-only multiplayer efforts like *Destiny*
- Strategy games like *Civilization VI*
- Quick-time choice driven cinematic mystery and horror story games like *Until Dawn*
- Handheld real-time augmented reality games like *Pokémon GO*

There's the *Sims*; the epic sweeping romance and action of *Mass Effect*; the intrepid puzzle-solving of *Tomb Raider's* Lara Croft and *Uncharted's* Nathan Drake; raucous multiplayer rounds of *Super Smash Brothers, Mortal Kombat,* and *Mario Kart;* the ever busy, ever building motion of *Minecraft*...The sheer scope of "digital games" is enormous, truly a field of tremendous possibility for an aspiring game developer. The work of creating digital games requires persistent curiosity and a drive to explore; perpetual mastery of new technology and refinement of creativity sustains game creators throughout long careers in the business of making play.

received entries from more than five thousand students of different ages, sexes, and ethnicities. At the local level, game jams in cities all over the United States and Canada offer opportunities for aspiring game developers of all ages and sexes to learn simple programming skills and create playable games.

MODDING

Another way to learn practical game-coding skills is to become involved in a modding community and experiment with games that provide open-source code for modders. A modder is someone who "modifies" an existing game, tweaking or adding new code to make additions and changes to a game that has made its source code available for the purpose. The *Elder Scrolls V: Skyrim,* for example, an open-world "sandbox" role-playing game in which the player has lots of choices when it comes to gameplay styles and objectives, has nurtured an extensive community of PC modders since its original release in 2011. With its high-definition re-release in 2016, the game's development company Bethesda allowed for unprecedented modding capability on Xbox One copies of the game, sparking mod-related interest among console players. One thing to keep in mind, however, is that hacking brand-name console hardware like your Xbox One, PlayStation 4, or Wii U is illegal and may result in heavy legal penalties. That's not the type of modding we're talking about here! All mentions of "modding" in

Software is a digital program you run on hardware. Hardware is the physical equipment you use to run virtual software programs.

this book refer to legal alterations made to games that release open-source code to players to allow them the fun of playing with the very makeup of the game itself.

Modding is a very hands-on way to get programming practice. Rather than attempting to program an entire game from scratch or build up a brand-new game using a game engine, modders get to start out with the code of a completed game and then change it to be more to their liking. A modder might remove a certain type of enemy they don't enjoy fighting, add extra non-player characters to a game environment, add or remove in-game resources, or give their character a brand new "skin" for a specialized look. By writing the appropriate code and uploading it along with the rest of the official code that makes up the game, a modder can add brand new environments to a game's map, or give the player godlike high-level powers or weapons unattainable in an un-modded game.

Modding communities tend to form around popularly modded games so that modders can share the results of their work with one another and learn and experiment together. Modding the game *Minecraft* is so popular that the game's wiki features an extensive community-generated tutorial to teach would-be modders to use the programming language Java to create *Minecraft* mods for any computer operating system. If a game that you enjoy provides support for modding, doing so is a good way to really get inside the guts of the game and see how what it's made of. Furthermore, successful mods (that is, mods that work well and add enjoyability to the game, not necessarily just popular mods) offer tangible proof of programming knowledge and experience for a would-be game programmer to display to potential hirers. Many people mod just for fun, but the hobby can greatly improve game programming skills and even potentially provide an opportunity to parlay those skills into professional employment with a game development team.

CHAPTER TWO

GAME DESIGN AND GAME ENGINES

G ame designers design games. That sounds really simple in those words, but it's a complicated, sometimes difficult task. Game design encompasses all components of a game: the objective of the game, the mechanics with which the player interacts with game objects and environments, and the methods by which a player achieves goals and advances through the game's levels or narrative. Game design combines the challenges of creativity with technical proficiency and problem solving. A game that *feels* incredibly simple from a player's perspective often requires an incredible amount of work on a designer's part to successfully invent, create, and implement. Game design is a field of study unto itself, and the production of complicated, collaborative games often separates the task into multiple roles overseen by a supervisor.

In 2009, veteran game designer Matt Allmer (who has worked for companies such as Electronic Arts,

Game design might seem like a solitary career, but it's not! Even indie designers who work alone rely on fellow developers to help them learn, create, critique, and promote their games.

Page 44 Studios, and Telltale Games) updated the classic "12 Principles of Animation" to create "The 13 Basic Principles of Game Design" for game development website Gamasutra. Allmer's points break down into categories of "Direction," "Behavior," "Progression," "Environment," "Method," and "Foundation," and he discusses techniques for directing the player's attention and action and enhancing narrative believability. He emphasizes the importance of physical effects and well-applied sounds in-game, offers suggestions as to the pacing of different games, addresses different processes for problem solving, and stresses the importance of clarity in communication. It's a lot to think about, and that's before you even consider the challenge of programming the game itself.

Some digital games are simple creations programmed by a single individual or small group of creators using a single programming language. Other games are enormous endeavors requiring massive amounts of code. In these cases, game developers often use programs called game engines to simplify the process of programming the game. A game engine already contains many complex combinations of code necessary to instruct a computer to perform specific actions common to certain types of digital games. A developer can therefore use a game engine to combine all of these elements together to build a game relatively quickly, rather than writing every bit of the code from scratch. As Michael Enger of gaming website Giant Bomb explains, "Game engines are great things, able to take the weight off developing a game idea to let you focus on the idea itself." However, knowledge of a game engine's particular programming language is nevertheless a major asset to a designer who may have to write new code to add a function not already included in the game engine's prewritten script or to edit code that isn't written precisely the way the game requires.

QUALITY ASSURANCE

Quality assurance testers get paid to play games for a living—but not to play casually for entertainment. QA testers try to break a game, basically: They seek out flaws, or "bugs," so that they can be fixed before the game is released to the paying public. Programming knowledge is very helpful to QA testers, allowing them to find the sources of problems and suggest solutions. Quality assurance testing can be a good entry into the field for relatively inexperienced developers who need to gain experience before stepping into a more advanced role on a dev team. Cara Ellison, a Scottish gaming journalist turned narrative

Games are made up of many interacting variables, and there's potential for something to go wrong at every step.

designer for AAA games such as *Dishonored 2*, began her career in the video game industry at the Edinburgh-based company Rockstar North, working on the QA team for *Grand Theft Auto IV*. In a 2015 interview for the website The Mary Sue, Ellison explained that quality assurance testers often go on to work in level design and programming, though she herself chose to apply the critical thinking skills she gained as a QA tester to the practice of writing games instead. "QA testers are just the internal game critics of the studio, really," she said. "They are very valuable."

GAME ENGINES

Game engines themselves are complex programs that take education and skill to operate. As Enger explained in his report for Giant Bomb, game engines are intended specifically to create games, rather than other applications, and their capabilities are specifically geared to that end. Game engines allow developers to control major elements of game design such as player input—the way a player controls in-game elements by clicking buttons on a controller, computer mouse, or keyboard or moves around the game environment using a joystick or buttons. A major feature of high-end game engines is their ability to power large graphics, such as detailed 3D environments (which are created in other specialized art programs, then "ported" or added to the game environment). Detailed graphics are made up of huge amounts of information that can be difficult for a computer to process quickly. Modern game engines, particularly those designed to create high-resolution 3D games, allow developers to not only add beautiful graphics to a game but also animate art assets with realistic lighting and motion effects.

Prewritten scripts for controlling the behavior of game objects and characters make life much easier for developers who would otherwise have to program the actions of every element in the game, and game engines also allow developers to incorporate physics to make objects in the game's environment move and react in predictable patterns. Game engines give a developer the option to incorporate sound into 3D games in immersive ways, "placing" sounds by modifying the volume relative to the player's position or adding muffled effects or echoes to give a realistic illusion of changing sound quality in different game environments. Game engines also greatly reduce the difficulty of incorporating networking functions in multiplayer games, letting developers focus on the design of online gameplay rather than forcing them to spend the bulk of their time working on the intricacies of enabling communication between different servers. (That's DevOps job anyway, as we'll discuss in a later section.)

However, not all game creation tools are this complicated. Other game development programs are geared toward creating 2D sidescrolling games or

Sometimes the simplest games hold up best over time. Their gameplay remains fun even as graphical capability and game complexity increase. Classic 2D Mario games remained popular today.

even text-based games that allow players to navigate through a narrative by choosing different options at conversational forks. SortingH.at is a tool created by indie game developer Zoë Quinn. It is an interactive guide that asks aspiring gamemakers to answer a number of questions regarding the sort of game they'd like to make, then provides a personalized list of resources for doing so. Pixel Prospector, also created by Quinn, provides a collection of useful resources for novice game makers, with a focus on game-making tools that do not require initial programming knowledge to use. The Games Are For Everyone website provides resources, not only to help aspiring game designers get started creating, but also to inform them about how to write critically about games, network with other gamemakers, distribute a game once it's completed, and possibly get hired to work at a game studio.

Game engines are extremely helpful tools for game developers, and, indeed, many large, complex AAA console games wouldn't be possible without them. However, there are drawbacks to using game engines to create games: because of their efficient pre-scripted features, they automatically place limits on designer creativity. As Michael Enger of Giant Bomb wrote, games built using the popular AAA game-building engine Unreal Engine 3 tend to have a very similar visual "feel," regardless of the different artwork and play styles of the games. Some developers, such as Tommy Refenes of *Super Meat Boy,* resent the creative limitation imposed by game engines and prefer to program their own games either partially or entirely. Programming knowledge comes in handy even for game designers who prefer to work with game engines, not only when it comes to customizing a game perfectly to a developer's specifications, but in making sure the game runs smoothly at all. Problems with a game's functionality, called bugs, must be fixed by figuring out where the problem is in the game's code and editing it to correct or work around the flaw. Without a thorough understanding of the particular programming language the game engine uses, a game designer could find him- or herself at a loss as to how to fix the game's problems.

CHAPTER THREE

ART AND ANIMATION

O n the surface, art might not sound like the most technical, programming-related aspect of game creation, and sometimes it's not. Simple 2D games might merely require scanned drawings to be ported in by a programmer, and text-based games might not require any artwork at all. In other cases, however, art is essential to a game's experience, and often its creation requires a great deal of technical proficiency.

TYPES OF ARTISTS

Concept artists create the look of game characters, objects, and environments, based on direction from a creative director. By using digital art programs to sculpt all of the shapes and surfaces with which the player interacts in a game, 3D modelers and texture artists impart a sense of believability and overall aesthetic cohesiveness. Animators are responsible for imbuing a game's characters and objects with the illusion of motion. Using specialty software, animators create libraries of different movements and, in collaboration with 3D modelers, apply them to various models. Technical artists, working in a relatively new role within the industry, bridge the gap between artists and programmers, combining programming proficiency with artistic skill to solve any problems that may arise from the attempt to integrate art elements into a game.

Renaud Galand became the lead character artist for Blizzard Entertainment, developer of the popular 2016 team-based multiplayer game *Overwatch*, after working for six years as a senior character artist with the company. As lead for the project, his responsibilities included not only working to direct

An enormous amount of effort and care goes into every aspect of the creation of iconic video game characters like Lara Croft.

the development of the entire character creation and implementation pipeline (including designing the look of the characters, creating initial prototypes, making 3D concept sculpts, and creating character models), but also interacting with other departments to ensure that everyone communicated smoothly and worked to translate the artwork smoothly from concept to playable game character. Prior to leading character art for Blizzard, Galand spent years working for smaller, lesser known game development companies, gaining experience in creating 2D promotional artwork and 3D environments, constructing polygonal models for 3D objects and characters, and providing high-resolution computer-generated and hand-painted textures for game objects and environments. A glance at Galand's résumé prior to his work with Blizzard might appear eclectic, but his meandering career path is not uncommon in the video game industry, where many people work in different roles on small development teams for little-known games to gain skills and make connections before securing a position on a larger project.

AUDIO ENGINEERING

Audio engineering is an enormous field in its own right, encompassing jobs such as music production, sound design, soundboard operation, and technical maintenance for recording studios and live bands. Audio engineers work in the music industry, in television, and in film. They're responsible for the sound quality of pretty much every professional piece of media you hear. When it comes to digital games, audio engineers create the "sound" of a game, layering a composer's music with sound effects, character voices, narration, and ambient atmospheric effects in order to provide an immersive atmosphere for hearing players. Audio is an incredibly important element of game design. If it's done well, the sound of a game might go nearly unnoticed by players, even as their mood and in-game actions are influenced by the things they hear. Bad sound design, on the other hand, can distract from an otherwise excellent game and ruin the player's sense of immersion.

As with most aspects of game creation, bigger, more complex games tend to have larger, more specialized sound teams, and different games employ different sound artists according to their particular requirements. *Overwatch*, for example, credits a nine-person sound department including a sound designer, voice-over producer, voice recordists, and several cinematic re-recording mixers. *The Sims 4's* sound department employed nearly the same number of people, but reconfigured, to include only one audio development director and multiple foley artists to create sound effects. Strategy game *Civilization VI* credits only one dialogue editor for sound, with a music department of three. In each case, the audio elements were carefully considered and tailored precisely to enhance each game's playing experience.

GAME VISUALS

Other artists take a different route to a career of creating game visuals. Dennis Hwang of Niantic Labs, the company behind *Pokémon GO*, interned at Google after graduating from college. When his bosses discovered that he had pursued an art major in school, they put him in charge of designing Google Doodles, the changing daily pictures incorporated into the logo on Google's homepage. Over a decade later, Hwang is now the director of visual design for all mobile games produced by Niantic Labs. The bright, simple, and fun graphics he and his team created for *Pokémon GO*

"Augmented reality" games use elements of reality to involve players in the game. In *Pokémon GO*, players have to walk around in real places in order to catch virtual monsters.

augment the experience of day-to-day reality for players all over the globe.

Final Fantasy XV lead animator Lluís Danti earned a multimedia engineering degree and master of arts in image synthesis and computer animation in his native Spain before beginning his professional career as a computer graphics animator in 2008. Since then he has worked in the United Kingdom, Japan, the Netherlands, and Canada, where he brought movement to the characters and cutscenes of *Final Fantasy XV* in 2016. Shawn Wilson, animator for *Titanfall 2*, first became interested in the illusion of motion when he watched the movie *Jurassic Park* as a kid. After gaining experience as an animator on movies such as 2011's *Alvin and the Chipmunks: Chipwrecked* and the more realistically styled 2012 fantasy film *Snow White and the Huntsman*, he moved on to working in video games and is now credited as lead animator for 2016's *Titanfall 2*.

A portfolio of work to demonstrate versatility and experience is essential for an aspiring game artist. Research the work of the artists credited on your favorite games; pay attention to their styles, the tricks of color, light and line they use to move the player's eye, and take note of the different software programs they use to create artwork for different titles. Befriending novice game designers who need artwork is a good way to gain practical experience creating original visuals for gameplay and also get practical experience at the work of communicating and collaborating with a designer. Anyone who wishes to work in art also needs to cultivate an ear for criticism and a willingness to rework an idea to benefit the finished product.

CHAPTER FOUR

LEVEL EDITORS: DIGITAL GAME DUNGEON MASTERS

Game designers envision a game's concept. Artists design the characters that populate a game based on a story written by narrative designers. Then animators and voice actors bring them to life. Level editors are video game architects: They design the environments players explore in-game, including landscapes, interiors, and objects. Level editors use game engines to create these virtual spaces and must possess a thorough knowledge of a game's programming language in order to make gameplay function smoothly in the environments they create.

LEVEL EDITORS

Level editors do some of the most wizardly work in video games. Their job is, essentially, to envision a place that doesn't exist, then manifest it in a virtual

LEARNING LEVEL DESIGN THROUGH PLAY

Games like *Super Mario Maker* put the power of game design in players' hands, making level editing a primary focus of gameplay.

You don't have to know how to code to start learning how to put together a video game level! *Super Mario Maker*, released for the Wii U console in autumn 2015, is designed around that exact premise: building Mario levels! In *Super Mario Maker*, the game itself basically acts as a game engine, letting players easily assemble 2D side-scrolling Mario game levels in the style of several different classic Mario games with different play styles and mechanics. Then, you can upload your masterpiece for others

(continued on the next page)

(continued from the previous page)

to play! There's just one catch. In a clever control designed to prevent the game's course world from becoming littered with broken, unplayable levels, *Super Mario Maker*'s designers inserted a condition: before you can upload a level for others to play, you must successfully play through and complete the course yourself. Mario isn't the only game franchise to overtly embrace game design as an aspect of gameplay. The *LittleBigPlanet* platformer series has provided players with a built-in level creator since its 2008 release and has continued to expand its players' creative scope, now allowing players to build not only platforming levels but shooting, fighting, racing, and sports games, even to create game cutscenes in its in-game level creator. *Minecraft*, released in 2009, revolves entirely around the concept of players gathering resources to rearrange, create, and re-edit game environments. Like *LittleBigPlanet* and *Super Mario Maker*, *Minecraft* cultivates a supportive community in which players share their work with one another, receive advice, criticisms, and praise and trade tips for building and modding. As mentioned in chapter one, any game that makes its source code publicly available can be "modded" by users with some knowledge of the game's programming language. Access to alter or add to a game's code allows players to act as level editors with the potential to create whole new areas to explore with new challenges to populate them.

space using code—and that's only the start of their task. Merely creating the world players move through in-game isn't enough. Building a level entails not only mapping the environment itself—a wall here, an unlockable door there, a stack of cubes the player might use as cover from enemy fire, maybe a lava pit or three—but also populating it with enemies and non-player characters, filling the space with little clues and carefully revealed bits of information to keep the player moving along. A level editor working on a 3D survival horror game might place a shining light to lure the player down a virtual hallway or conceal a hidden bonus in a far dark corner of an environment. In 2D sidescrolling games, players are conditioned to move toward the right of the screen to progress toward their goal. But if the level designer wants the player to climb up, they'll include some sort of clue to direct the player's progress through the space, like a ladder, climbing rope, a netlike texture to give the player the hint, or even an arrow pointing toward the top of the screen. The level editor must decide where to place obstacles and enemies, seeking a delicate balance to make sure the gameplay is challenging and fun for the player, but not so hard that it becomes punishing and makes the player want to give up. Level editors choose where to place energy refills and health packs, new ammunition, and helpful items of all kinds. Level editors also help to weave a game's story together properly, choosing where and how to reveal narrative texts and tidbits that advance a game's plot or add detail to its world. A level editor has to get inside the player's

The pace and flow of gameplay is essential to fast-paced multiplayer shooters like *Titanfall 2*. Level editors' work is essential to ensuring fun, satisfying play experiences.

head and figure out how to guide her throughout the game without being too obvious, to give her the information and items she needs at exactly the right time to best unfold the narrative and keep her attention invested, and to motivate the player to keep performing a series of repetitive button presses for hours, for *fun*, all before the game even exists yet. Wizardly work, indeed.

Level editors also work to fix all of the problems that crop up over the course of their labor. They might be asked to rearrange their work to accommodate ideas from other members of the development team. They might learn that part of their level is difficult to understand from a quality tester's perspective and be forced to rethink their design. They might work on an entire level and perfect it, only to find it cut from the game because of space constraints! Mostly, they might discover that their level is full of bugs—glitches that disturb the game and impede player progress. When bugs appear, level editors have to search through the game's code to locate the source of the problem and create a fix for it. When bugs happen (and they always happen), somebody has to understand the programming language the code is written in to repair mistakes or implement a "patch," or workaround solution.

CHAPTER FIVE

NARRATIVE DESIGN

Narrative designers create the story told throughout the course of a game, devising a plot that coordinates with level design and gameplay mechanics. These writers may use programming software to construct branching dialogue that changes depending upon a player's choices and must ensure that the typically brief amount of character interaction in cinematic cutscenes between play offers sufficient explanation to fill the player in on plot developments without becoming repetitive or confusing. Narrative designers also supply various written material inserted throughout the game, such as supplementary world-building material (journals, letters) and tutorial explanation text. Narrative designers must consider how the story informs and drives gameplay, a puzzle that requires a strong understanding of game construction.

Game plots can seem silly or even downright nonsensical when considered separately from the context of play, but game writing is actually a carefully honed art.

CREATING A NARRATIVE

Angel Leigh McCoy, fiction writer and narrative designer for text-based roleplaying games at companies such as White Wolf and Wizards of the Coast and a narrative and lore designer for the online multiplayer roleplaying game *Guild Wars 2*, wrote a 2016 blog post for the game development website Gamasutra discussing important considerations for narrative designers. As McCoy explains, "creating narrative for a video game has similar challenging, frustrating, and fun elements as those you encounter when putting together a jigsaw puzzle. Both tasks require critical thinking and the ability to see the big picture as well as the details." First, does the story support and strengthen the game's brand? Does it make sense to the player? Do the story elements serve and even exceed player expectations? Story elements must conform to the rules and physics of the game's world. For example, if a character is suddenly able to teleport, the narrative designer must provide a reason for the ability that makes sense within the laws of the game's universe. Otherwise the choice will break the "rules" of the game and wreck the player's suspension of disbelief. A narrative designer must be able to take ideas from other members of the development team—the director, level designers, the artists—and weave them successfully into the game's story. In other cases, the narrative designer might determine that an idea is incompatible with other game elements or plotlines and communicate the problem to the rest of the team. Narrative designers must not only create a game's story, but consider whether or not certain ideas have been best implemented, decide whether or not plots are necessary to the game or series' advancement, and construct plot in such a way to allow future story developments to unfold believably.

A narrative designer might work on a large AAA game development team, bearing responsibility for balancing different team members' concerns and weaving story elements together in a sensible fashion or could be the sole game developer responsible for every aspect of an indie game! In any case, a narrative designer can't do a good job without thorough consideration of all aspects of game design. Cara Ellison, a member of the narrative design team for the game *Dishonored 2*, began her career in video games as a quality assurance tester for Rock Star's *GTA IV,* gaining knowledge about the process of game making by searching for flaws and envisioning improvements for a large game in its testing stage. Ellison then took the communication skills she'd gained earning a university degree in English literature and began writing critically about games for sites such as Rock Paper Shotgun and Kotaku. In 2014, Ellison traveled around the world living with indie game developers and interviewing them about their processes for a series of essays she eventually compiled into a book called *Embed with Games*. A narrative-driven indie game she made called *Sacrilege* caught the attention of Arkane Studios designer Harvey Smith and, after a grueling round of writing tests and interviews, she combined the experience and knowledge she'd built over the past years to earn a job on the narrative design team for 2015's *Dishonored 2* and a number of other games yet to be released. "I guess if you want to work in games development in any meaningful way, you have to be making games and be interested in the process of making games," she said in a 2015 interview with The Mary Sue. "Even when I got a job in Quality Assurance we were encouraged to take part in the process of creating the game by giving ideas and feedback." This experience, followed by several years of thinking and writing games criticism and observing

Effective individuals who work in game development are typically interested in all aspects of game creation, not just their own specialties.

and writing about indie game designers at work, eventually prepared Ellison to step into a role developing dialogue and in-game texts for the *Dishonored* franchise. Ellison's advice to aspiring game writers? "Go to some Unity [game engine] classes, I think, and learn the basics of how to script. You could do what I did and pick up a simple text game engine like Twine to play around with narrative design—I think the people over at Telltale prototype narrative in Twine too. Also: find a mentor and a gamemaking partner! Ask questions! Mess around. Experiment. If you start making games with other people it's a better experience and problems are solved so much quicker."

VISUAL NOVELS

A visual novel is sort of an interactive, mixed media comic book experience: the player moves through a series of static frames animated with text and sound effects in order to progress the story. Driven by storytelling, rather than complex gameplay mechanics, visual novels often make use of branching storylines, requiring the player to go through the game multiple times in order to experience each of the game's possible endings. Though their mechanics may be simple and gameplay minimalistic, visual novels are often critically hailed for their riveting stories. Unrestrained by the narrative limitations imposed by other styles of gameplay like puzzle games, platformers, fighting games, and first person shooters, visual novels offer a would-be creator near-unlimited scope for imagination and give the player an opportunity to experience a truly innovative story experience enhanced by artwork and voice acting performances.

BRINGING CODING SKILLS TO STORYTELLING

Coding skills are helpful to narrative designers because a thorough understanding of a game's

Some fans show their appreciation for game characters with cosplay. Others write fan fiction, inventing their own plots for favorite game characters.

underlying construction allows writers to better understand and best use the framework upon which the narrative is built. Twine, a popular "open-source tool for telling interactive, nonlinear stories," as its website explains, allows would-be narrative designers with minimal HTML coding skills to create branching dialogue-based games—choose-your-own adventure style experiences in which a player's choice at each juncture will influence the events and outcome of the game. BioWare, the Toronto-based development company behind the *Dragon Age* and *Mass Effect* roleplaying franchises, encourages writing team applicants to submit Twine-created narratives in order to demonstrate their ability to weave engaging branching dialogue and show that they can master some basic coding skills. Writing a Twine game (or fifty) is a great way for aspiring narrative designers to gain experience in creating believable branching story sequences while building a portfolio to show off their creativity and skill.

CHAPTER SIX

DEVOPS ENGINEERING

Many digital games feature online multiplayer gameplay that functions separately from the game's single-player narrative—in online only games like *Destiny*, that's the whole point! DevOps engineers are responsible for creating and maintaining networks for online play, often across multiple platforms—an extremely complicated task. DevOps engineers are expert programmers and web developers, capable of coordinating with different elements of a game development team to maintain efficiency and security and solve problems quickly. DevOps is a unique, rapidly growing field within the business of digital game making and distributing.

DEVOPS AGILITY

"Agile" is the adjective of choice for DevOps experts when it comes to describing their intended role in the

DevOps engineers protect gamers from potential security breaches and work to make real-time online multiplayer platforms stable and convenient for players.

digital game industry. "Traditional models of development can introduce artificial process boundaries where you have product management handing off requirements to devs who hand off code to QA who hand off additional code to Ops, and then everyone hopes that at the end it is going to work," explained Allison Miller, Electronic Arts' senior director of operations, in a 2013 interview with *Wired* magazine. The purpose of a DevOps team is to bridge the gaps between different departments in a large company, protecting the publisher's digital platform from online

TECHNOLOGY AND CHANGING GOALPOSTS

Like any technology-based enterprise, the digital game industry is constantly evolving based on innovation and increasing technological capability. People who wish to work in games must recognize that they will probably spend their careers perpetually chasing inventive ways to use ever-improving technology. Sometimes their efforts fail, and on other occasions they may succeed but find their work thwarted by unlucky timing or changing corporate policy. Fortunately for the future fun of gamers everywhere, people who are drawn to coding and game-making often thrive on a cycle of failure, repetition, and improvement, using the lessons they learn to continually approach problems in fresh and ever more effective ways. Curious, competitive, challenge-hungry problem solvers are consistently in demand in the business of game making. Their motivation and risk-taking work enables everyone else's leisure-time play.

attack by hackers and ensuring that customers can pay for and play the company's games safely and conveniently, 24/7. DevOps engineers dedicate their skill and ingenuity to making online gameplay immediate, satisfying, and safe for players, and if they succeed in their goals, their work is largely invisible to the gamers who benefit from their efforts.

Miller herself did not enter the video game industry as a developer. Rather, she began her career working in fraud prevention and e-commerce, designing and building threat deterrence and prevention systems for online payment system companies like PayPal and Visa before joining EA in 2012. The digital transformation that began at EA at the turn of the decade drew Miller's interest, and the challenge of creating a successful cross-platform digital game delivery and play service appealed to her ambition. DevOps is a job for coders who are intellectually curious and hungry for challenge, as the aims of

DevOps is the security force of online multiplayer games, making sure players can make payments easily and access games immediately, safe from the threat of hackers.

the work continually fluctuate according to the individual company and its ever-changing needs. DevOps engineers also basically work to make themselves unnecessary, automating processes to streamline systems and speed efficiency wherever possible.

"We evaluate every transaction that goes through our e-commerce flows to see if it meets our requirements for good customers or if it fits a pattern that we know is associated with fraud. That system needs to be smart and fast, and needs to be always on. We use a combination of cloud-based and internal tools for this scoring/evaluation process, and a lot of behavioral analytics, statistics, and experimentation with machine learning techniques," Miller told *Wired*. Miller's team personally designs systems processes and performs their own coding, testing, and implementation to make sure everything performs as intended before, during, and after game releases. Programmers, protectors, uninterrupted gameplay providers: DevOps engineers are the unsung heroes of online gameplay.

CHAPTER SEVEN

CRUNCH: HOW GAMES GET MADE

Game developers make games and then get paid, right? Well, not exactly. The field of digital games is huge, encompassing an immense variety of games. Games are marketed and sold very differently. Massively multiplayer online roleplaying games like *World of Warcraft* charge players an upfront price for the game software, then a recurring monthly fee in order to access the game's servers and play with friends. Mobile games like *Pokémon GO* are free to play, but earn money from microtransactions: inexpensive payments players exchange for in-game conveniences such as increased inventory capacity and extra resources. Indie game developers publish games on Steam to sell their creations to PC, Mac, and Linux-using gamers. Large studios of developers are funded by deep-pocketed publishers to create big-name exclusive triple-A, or AAA games for video game consoles like Xbox One and PlayStation 4. These

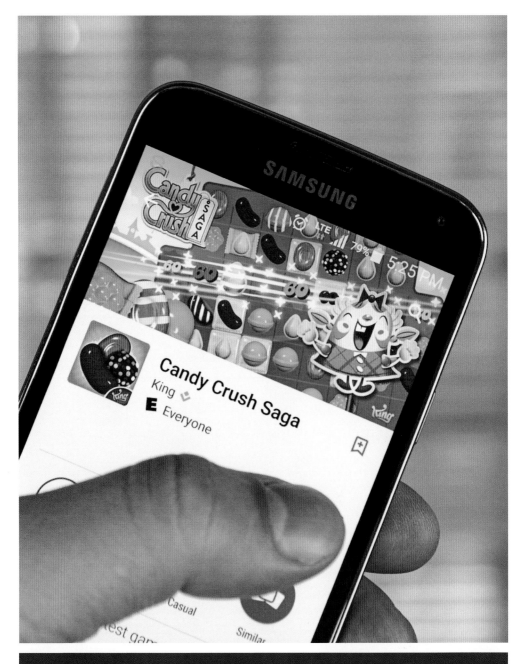

Many mobile games earn revenue through microtransactions, small payments players make to buy in-game items or advance quickly through levels without having to wait.

games are extremely expensive to make, and their publishers depend upon huge sales figures to recoup their investments.

STARTING OUT

Creating play for a living can, ironically, be a stressful job at all levels of game development. Aspiring game makers may find it difficult to break into their desired position in the digital game industry. Hard work for little or no payment is typical when a game dev is starting out; it's hard to get hired without experience, and it's hard to get experience without doing work. Successful video game devs are typically persistent and prolific, willing to "grind" at their tasks like a player working to gain XP in a fantasy game. A portfolio of work that demonstrates necessary skills is requisite for earning a job at an established game development studio of any size, and creating an impressive body of work is a difficult undertaking, particularly when it doesn't pay yet. Even when a new developer manages to get hired at a famous company earning a comfortable salary, the work is still quite demanding. In the best of cases, making games is a difficult process of brainstorming, creating, making mistakes, hitting dead ends, and reconfiguring to find solutions.

CRUSHING CRUNCH AND BOOSTING COLLABORATIVE CULTURE

Some developers view crunch— to cram a lot of extra work into a short amount of time—as a necessary evil, an unpleasant reality of the process of making video games. In contrast, other studios such as Double Fine, creators of the upcoming *Psychonauts 2*, actively work to correct damaging industry practices and develop a nurturing, diverse work culture. "Double Fine is deeply committed to the work/life balance of every employee. We value team members' important commitments outside of the company. We support flexible hours, working from home, and an open paid time off policy to help them take care of those commitments," the company president and chief executive officer Tim Schafer wrote in an open letter to prospective employees posted to the company's website in November 2016. This commitment to promoting employee health, safety, and happiness signals a shift in the broader culture of the business of making digital games, toward preserving and encouraging creativity rather than burning out passion with overwork."We want our perspectives to always be challenged—to benefit our team's quality of life," Schafer explained, "and also the quality of our games." Funomena, an independent game studio in San Francisco, was founded by Robin Hunicke and Martin Middleton after they worked together on the acclaimed 2012 PlayStation Network title *Journey*. After three years of commitment to a philosophy and workflow dedicated to a productive balance of work, life, and what the company's founders describe as "meaningful play," the company has grown to employ fifteen people and still actively searches to add new talent to its roster. "We are working to build a deliberately developmental organization where we make beautiful, unique and experimental games," states Funomena's company philosophy. "We seek collaborators who have a growth mindset, and are willing to experiment, fail and learn from their mistakes."

THE DOWNSIDE OF THE GAMES INDUSTRY

In 2004, game designer Erin Hoffman wrote an explosive online exposé about working conditions at the video game publisher Electronic Arts (EA), where her significant other was then employed. Under the pseudonym "EA Spouse," Hoffman revealed that the company unethically exploited her partner for illegal amounts of labor without adequate recompense, enforcing an unhealthy "crunch"-driven work schedule that was destructive to employees' health and relationships. Unfortunately, as a 2015 report by Jason Schreier of Kotaku revealed, the same culture of overwork continues to prevail in the video game industry

Making games is fun, but it's also hard work. Game developers must prioritize their health and maintain responsible work schedules to avoid burnout.

more than a decade later, plaguing everyone from indie developers to AAA teams.

Development companies "crunch"—cram a lot of extra work into a short amount of time—for a variety of reasons. Often, the publisher financing a game will demand last-minute changes from a game development company. Rather than ask the publisher for more money or time or cut promised game features to complete the project—a risky maneuver for a development studio, particularly if they depend on their publisher to fund future games and keep everyone employed—a studio head will often choose to squeeze salaried workers for unpaid overtime. This wouldn't be a problem if crunch were a rarely used, last-resort solution only for major problems in game development. Unfortunately, as Schreier wrote in 2015, "In the world of video games, many producers and directors see mandatory overtime not as a contingency plan but as a natural part of game development, to be regularly used as a way to cut costs and make the most ambitious games on the shortest schedules." Small development studios rely on crunch because they'll run out of money otherwise. Big dev studios crunch to meet changing publisher demands and tight deadlines. As positions at game development studios are highly competitive and in-demand, however, individual employees find themselves forced to comply with unhealthy extended unpaid working hours in order to complete their assigned tasks. If the publisher pulls funding for the project, the dev team risks being laid off, and thus crunch culture has persisted for more than a decade after the broader gaming community first became aware of its dangers.

Fortunately, evolving technology has provided some relief for overpressured studio game developers. Today, the ability to remotely patch mistakes and provide post-release downloadable content takes a bit of the weight off of exhausted dev teams' shoulders, allowing them to address any mistakes that persist through the game's release even after the title ships. At the same time, new possibilities lead to additional work: it has now become common for development teams to continue work on supplemental down-loadable content for months after a game becomes available to the public. "By nature, game developers are creative, ambitious people with a habit of biting off more than they can chew. It's hard to envision a video game industry where people aren't over-promising things," Schreier explained in his report to Kotaku.

CHAPTER EIGHT

NETWORKING

I f you want to work in the video game industry, networking is essential. Not "networking" as in maintaining stable servers for online play (though that's important, too), but the type of in-person, real human interaction-based "networking" of meeting peers, making contacts, and forming relationships with professionals in the field. It's a vital qualification for any job on a video game dev team: you have to work well with others. People tend to hire people they know, or know by good reputation, because they want to assemble compatible teams that will work together cohesively to create a great product. Good behavior and genuine enthusiasm for game making impresses future coworkers and earns jobs, even though it may take persistence.

The annual *Game Career Guide* issued by professional game industry site Gamasutra emphasizes the importance of networking—attending industry

Game creation is a collaborative endeavor. To be successful at any career within the digital games industry, you have to play well with others.

conferences and making friends, mentors, and professional connections in the industry—to finding game development jobs. Networking was a theme in the 2016 *Game Career Guide,* including a section titled "Breaking in the Easy(ish) Way! How Attending Expos Can Land You a Job." Written by Brandon Sheffield, editor-in-chief of *Game Developer* magazine and senior contributing editor at Gamasutra, the piece (which is available in full online) tells the stories of four individuals who work in different areas of the video game industry. The piece also includes what they did prior to breaking into the field professionally, the steps they took toward reaching their goals, and the relationships they fostered within the industry that eventually led to work. Lara, a student and aspiring game developer, has attended the E3 (Electronic Entertainment Expo) conference for free since 2013 through a program that allows students to do a set amount of conference work in exchange for a pass and made a friend who later served as a valuable reference when she applied for (and scored) a Robot Chicken internship. Jarryd made a major career shift from managing servers and infrastructures for a large

Networking is all about making friendly professional connections. Getting to know professional peers is a worthy undertaking itself, and if a friendship happens to lead to a job opportunity, great!

bank to full-time game development after attending the Game Developer's Conference (GDC). The experience introduced him to people who showed him that the coding skills he already possessed qualified him for interesting work in game development, setting him on a path to a packed full-time dev career. "Sometimes focusing on making a friend or connection before focusing on getting a job prospect can lead to opportunities you may have missed otherwise," he advises.

Jesse, a music composer, traveled to GDC decades ago with the express intent of attending the job fair. Introducing himself from booth to booth, asking each company if they outsourced the music for their games, he discovered that LucasArts was looking to hire a staff composer. He didn't get the job, but kept his spirits up and returned to GDC the following year, making a point to check in with LucasArts to let them know what he'd been up to and tell them that he was still interested in working with them if an opportunity became available. Eight months later, a position did indeed come open and Jesse's contacts at LucasArts called him in to interview for the job, which he landed! He went on to work for years as LucasArts' in-house sound designer and a composer on games like *Star Wars: The Old Republic*, *Marvel's Avengers Academy, and CounterSpy*. Illustrator Del gained steady work after befriending a group of game music composers at her first Game Developer's Conference. As she later put it, "I'd made some incredible friends, and friends know friends who could use an artist!"

GAINING EXPERIENCE

Experience is the most important qualification for game development jobs. Small independent prototypes created at game jams or during free time do more to show off a developer's skill and creativity to potential hirers than an extensive academic résumé. Group-produced game credits demonstrate the ability to work with a team. It's important for anyone interested in game development to keep track of work accomplished, even if it's not professional. If you're an artist, potential employers will want to see a portfolio of your work—not just to see that you're good at the artwork and do it well, but to see that you like doing the work, that you produce new artwork regularly and continue to evolve and improve. If you're an aspiring narrative designer, you want to build up an impressive body of written work to attest to your dedication and demonstrate your voice as a writer. And if you want to be a programmer? Get to coding!

Valuable experience comes not only from successful efforts, but perhaps even more so from failures, which tend to inspire creative problem solving—a highly valued skill when it comes to game design. Anyone who wishes to turn their coding skill to game development must be prepared to face failure to attempt to outwit unexpected problems, and sometimes to fail completely. When a game developer keeps at it, however, and wins? Sometimes they get the privilege of creating a whole new world.

MAKING GOOD CONNECTIONS

Networking isn't about being inauthentic or just trying to meet as many people as possible. It's definitely not about spamming potential employers with shallow self-promotion or messaging a busy person with updates so often that you make yourself a nuisance. Instead, it's sort of like job dating. Making genuine connections with people you respect leads to positive potential coworking experiences. If you don't get a job right away? Big deal! You made a friend or a

A good attitude goes a long way both in digital games and in the real-world career of making them. Be nice!

connection with someone you admire! As people who like to play games (and especially people who work at making games) know, persistence is key. Cheerful willingness to try again, or try another solution, and to keep moving forward in the face of difficulty while maintaining a good attitude are coveted qualities in anyone who hopes to join a game development team.

GLOSSARY

AAA The industry term for highly funded, blockbuster console games.

animator A person who uses specialty software to give game characters and objects the believable illusion of movement.

audio engineer The person who records sounds for a game and weaves sound effects and music together to create a cohesive, engaging overall "sound" for the game.

bugs Mistakes or problems in a game's code.

code A collection of languages in which computer programs are written.

crunch Forced overtime work with the goal of releasing a game by deadline.

cutscene An in-game cinematic, often used to provide narrative information about the game's plot.

DevOps engineer A person who creates and maintains secure networks for online play.

game developer A person who works in the creative industry of video game production, designing, programming, or working in some other aspect toward the creation of a playable game.

game engine A specialty software program that allows a game developer to build levels without having to write every part of the code for each element and script.

indie Short for "independent," indie game developers and studios work on small, unique games that don't require as much oversight as the production of AAA games.

level editor A developer who creates game environments and populates them with obstacles, enemies, and rewards.

narrative designer The strategist and writer of a game's plot, who may also write dialogue and supplementary world-building materials.

networking Meeting people and building relationships with people who work in your industry in order to learn from them and make contacts for future job opportunities.

programmer A developer who writes the code for a video game.

programming language A formal computer language designed to communicate instructions to a machine.

quality assurance testing The quality assurance, or "QA" team, plays early versions of the game in order to locate bugs and provide feedback on player perspective.

texture artist The person who creates "skins" and surfaces to cover frameworks built by 3D modelers.

3D modeler A person who uses specialty software to sculpt the figures and objects in a game.

video game console A hardware device created for the purpose of playing video games on a TV screen, like Nintendo Wii U, Xbox One, or PlayStation 4.

Bethesda Softworks

1370 Piccard Drive
Rockville, MD 20850
(301) 926-8300
Website: https://bethesda.net/en
Located in Maryland, this thirty-year-old game development company produces *The Elder Scrolls* roleplaying games.

BioWare

200-4445 Calgary Trail NW
Edmonton, AB T6H 5R7
Canada
(780) 430-0164
Website: http://www.bioware.com/en
The Canada-based arm of the large game development company BioWare produces internationally famous roleplaying game series such as *Mass Effect* and *Dragon Age*.

Blizzard Entertainment

PO Box 18979
Irvine, CA 92623
(949) 955-1382
Website: http://us.blizzard.com/en-us
This game development company creates and supports *World of Warcraft* games.

Capybara Games

174 Spadina Avenue, Suite 401

Toronto, ON M5T 2C2
Canada
(416) 533-6649
Website: http://www.capybaragames.com
This independent game studio is based in Toronto,
    Canada, and makes iPhone, Nintendo DS, and
    downloadable console games.

Double Fine Productions
525 Brannan Street, Suite 200
San Francisco, CA 94107
(415) 896-1110
Website: http://www.doublefine.com
This American game development company promotes
    diversity in hiring.

Funomena
398 5th Street
San Francisco, CA 94107
(773) 251-0984
Website: http://www.funomena.com
This experiment-driven American indie game develop-
    ment studio explores the artistry of play.

WEBSITES

Because of the changing nature of internet links, Rosen
Publishing has developed an online list of websites
related to the subject of this book. This site is updated
regularly. Please use this link to access the list:

http://www.rosenlinks.com/CYP/gaming

FOR FURTHER READING

Dobre, Adrian, and Dev Ramtal. *Physics for Flash Games, Animation, and Simulations*. New York, NY: Springer, 2011.

Ellison, Cara. *Embed with Games: A Year on the Couch with Game Developers*. Edinburgh, Scotland: Polygon Books, 2015.

Fullerton, Tracy. *Game Design Workshop: A Playcentric Approach to Creating Innovative Games*. Boca Raton, FL: CRC Press, 2014.

Koster, Raph. *A Theory of Fun for Game Design*. Scottsdale, AZ: Paraglyph Press, 2004.

Rettig, Pascal. *Professional HTML5 Mobile Game Development*. Indianapolis, IN: John Wiley & Sons Inc., 2012.

Rogers, Scott. *Level Up! The Guide to Great Video Game Design*. West Sussex, UK: John Wiley & Sons Ltd., 2014.

Schell, Jesse. *The Art of Game Design: A Book of Lenses*. Boca Raton, FL: CRC Press, 2015.

Shah, Ryan. *Master the Art of Unreal Engine 4*. Devon, UK: Kitatus Studios, 2014.

Tristem, Ben, and Mike Geig. *Unity Game Development in 24 Hours, Sams Teach Yourself*. Indianapolis, IN: Pearson Education, 2016.

Unger, Kimberly, and Jeannie Novak. *Game Development Essentials: Mobile Game Development*. Clifton Park, NY: Delmar Cengage Learning, 2012.

Allmer, Matt. "The 13 Basic Principles of Gameplay Design." Gamasutra, February 27, 2009. http://www.gamasutra.com/view/feature/132341/the_13_basic_principles_of_.php.

Bogdan, Greg. "Top 7 Programming Languages Used in Video Games." Freelancer.com, February 9, 2016. https://www.freelancer.com/community/articles/top-7-programming-languages-used-in-video-games.

Colao, JJ. "Codecademy Raises $10 Million To Conquer The World." Forbes, June 19, 2012. http://www.forbes.com/sites/jjcolao/2012/06/19/codecademy-raises-10-million-to-conquer-the-world/#147a51c29b40.

Enger, Michael. "Game Engines: How Do They Work?" Giant Bomb, June 20, 2013. http://www.giantbomb.com/profile/michaelenger/blog/game-engines-how-do-they-work/101529/.

Fissenden, Emma. "Game Changer: Dishonored 2's Cara Ellison on Experimenting with Narrative Design, Owning Your Talent & the Importance of Self-Care." The Mary Sue, July 21, 2015. http://www.themarysue.com/game-changer-cara-ellison.

Galand, Renaud. "Renaud Galand, Lead Character Artist at Blizzard Entertainment." LinkedIn. Retrieved November 5, 2016. https://www.linkedin.com/in/renaudgaland.

"Getting Started with UE4." Unreal Engine User Tutorials, Epic Games. Retrieved November 21, 2016. https://docs.unrealengine.com/latest/INT/GettingStarted/index.html.

Goode, Lauren. "Seven Questions for Pokémon Go Designer Dennis Hwang." The Verge, November 1, 2016. http://www.theverge.com/2016/11/1/13483768/dennis-hwang-pokemon-go-designer-google-doodle.

Groc, Isabelle. "DevOps at the Gate: An Interview with EA's Allison Miller." Wired, July 2013. https://www.wired.com/insights/2013/07/devops-at-the-gate-an-interview-with-eas-senior-director-of-operations-allison-miller.

Hayes, Jason. "The Code/Art Divide: How Technical Artists Bridge The Gap." Gamasutra, August 20, 2008. http://www.gamasutra.com/view/feature/130074/the_codeart_divide_how_technical_.php.

McCoy, Angel Leigh. "8 Questions That Improve Your Game's Narrative." Gamasutra, October 24, 2016. http://www.gamasutra.com/blogs/AngelLeighMcCoy/20161024/283602/8_Questions_That_Improve_Your_Games_Narrative.php.

O'Dell, J. "Tackling Tech's Gender Problem the Right Way: Teaching Women to Code." VentureBeat, January 10, 2013. http://venturebeat.com/2013/01/10/hackbright.

Refenes, Tommy. "How Do I Get Started Programming Games?" Gamasutra Blogs, January 7, 2013. http://www.gamasutra.com/blogs/TommyRefenes/20130107/184432/How_do_I_get_started_programming_games.php.

Schreier, Jason. "The Horrible World of Video Game Crunch." Kotaku, September 26, 2016. http://

kotaku.com/crunch-time-why-game-developers-work-such-insane-hours-1704744577.

Sheffield, Brandon. "Breaking in the Easy(ish) Way!" Game Developer Magazine 2016 Gamer Career Guide, July 2016. http://dc.ubm-us.com/i/702705-2016-game-career-guide/7?m4=.

Team Bios. Respawn Entertainment. Retrieved November 21, 2016. http://www.respawn.com/team.

INDEX

ABOUT THE AUTHOR

Jennifer Culp is a lifelong video game enthusiast. She writes nonfiction science and tech books for teens.

PHOTO CREDITS

Cover Edge Magazine/Future/Getty Images; p. 1 (background) Verticalarray/Shutterstock.com; p. 5 CREATISTA/Shutterstock.com; p. 9 Vintage Tone/ Shutterstock.com; p. 15 Future Publishing/Getty Images; pp. 18, 33, 64 Bloomberg/Getty Images; p. 20 Boston Globe/Getty Images; p. 23 © iStockphoto.com/ ilbusca; pp. 26–27 David McNew/Getty Images; p. 30 Matthew Corley/Shutterstock.com; p. 36 Yuya Shino/ Getty Images; p. 39 Przemek Tokar/Shutterstock.com; pp. 42–43 Chesnot/Getty Images; p. 45 Brook Mitchell/ Getty Images; p. 48 © iStockphoto.com/borealisgal- lery; pp. 50–51 © iStockphoto.com/andresr; p. 54 dennizn/Shutterstock.com; p. 58 © iStockphoto.com/ DragonImages; pp. 62–63 g-stockstudio/Shutterstock.com; p. 67 © iStockphoto.com/AzmanJaka; interior background pages graphics pp. 8, 17, 25, 32, 38, 47, 53, 61 (angry birds) Nieuwland/Shutterstock.com, (binary code) Titima Ongkantong/Shutterstock.com.

Designer: Michael Moy
Editor and Photo Researcher: Bethany Bryan